you're graduating
college + start
life! I'm so p
olly, you ha
strong head
shoulders. I

true-blue
friends

true-blue
friends

CARMEN RENEE BERRY
AND TAMARA TRAEDER

**Andrews McMeel
Publishing**

Kansas City

Book design by Susan Hood
Book composition by Holly Camerlinck

ISBN: 0-7407-0087-1
Library of Congress Catalog Card Number: 99-65533

The text of this book was previously published in *girlfriends* by Carmen Renee Berry and Tamara Traeder (Wildcat Canyon Press, 1995).

What do we live for, if
it is not to make life less
difficult for each other?

—GEORGE ELIOT
(MARY ANN EVANS)

Paying Attention

I ALWAYS FELT THAT THE GREAT HIGH PRIVILEGE, RELIEF, AND COMFORT OF FRIENDSHIP WAS THAT ONE HAD TO EXPLAIN NOTHING.

—*Katherine Mansfield*

Deep friendships often result in knowing, frequently without asking, what the other feels and needs. Somehow our psyches become intertwined, and we know things about each other that we have no rational reason to know—no one told us, it's not written down anywhere. Of course, we may not always know all of the whys and wherefores, but we get the sense that something is wrong, and we find out the details.

8

Not only can women friends know what will comfort us, they also can know just what we need to hear about daily matters. As Elizabeth, a homemaker and mother of three from southern Missouri, writes, "Women are so busy being all things to all people, especially their families, that few men, children, and coworkers are aware of their needs. But unlike most males I have come into contact with, close female friends notice everything. They

compliment you when you've had your hair cut. They notice a new outfit. They acknowledge weight loss and ignore additional pounds. They are also intuitively aware when something's wrong yet won't press until you're ready to tell."

Even young girlfriends experience this attentive bond with each other, as seventeen-year-old Molly says of her friend, who is also named Molly, "You get more comfortable with each other. We're so close now it's like we read each other's minds. It's kind of weird."

Ellen, a West Coast psychologist, told us about the comfort she experienced when her friends attended to her during her mother's terminal illness. She said, "When my mother was dying, she lived in Georgia. My brother lives there, too; he was taking care of her, and I would fly to Georgia and stay with him while we cared for her. She was in intensive care for

almost two months, and then a series of crises
followed. I would fly to Georgia and then she
10 would stabilize, so I'd go back home. There was
a lot of back and forth. It was very stressful.

"Some of my friends, Janine and Maria
and some others, put together this care pack-
age of all my favorite things at that time—
books and tapes and foods and all kinds of
things—and mailed it to my brother's house
in Georgia for me. It was very lovely."

Colette, now in her late thirties, tells the
story of a painful period in life when she
found herself pregnant by an unsympathetic
and uncaring man. "I'd told some of my
friends that things were kind of rough, but I
was embarrassed that I was in a relationship
where I was in love like a teenager and it was

not working. Here I thought it was the real thing and I wasn't being treated well. When I got pregnant I decided to get an abortion, but I didn't tell any friends about my situation, except for one, and that was not until right before I went in for the abortion. When I came home, there were flowers on the table and a note from her saying all the good stuff about me—how I had always been able to hear things and not be judgmental, and other things. Something like that went so far to help me in that period of my life."

Understanding what our friends need isn't magic. It comes from our taking the time to notice one another and respond

to the needs we see or sometimes only intuit. Diane Sawyer sums it up succinctly: "I think 12 the one thing that I have learned is that there is no substitute for paying attention."[1] Many women have been raised not to talk about their needs, not to complain if something is wrong, so friends who pay attention to our needs are especially precious. We all appreciate when someone notices we are hurting.

This kind of attentiveness takes effort, and a real girlfriend makes the effort.

1. Quoted in *The Quotable Woman* (Philadelphia: Running Press, 1991), 122.

Would I Have Made It Without You?

I OFTEN THINK, HOW COULD I HAVE
SURVIVED WITHOUT THESE WOMEN?
—*Claudette Renner*

Looking back on childhood friendships
caused some of the women we interviewed
to realize just how important those friendships were in surviving difficult family situations. Layer upon layer of experiences
teaches us about ourselves and one another.
The burnishing and polishing of life's events
creates a fine glowing vessel of friendship.

Cynthia, a grocery clerk in Southern California, describes the richness that her lifelong friendship with Carmen has provided: "We have known each other since we were ten. We would see each other on Sundays at church and sometimes spend the afternoons together. I don't think we knew how dysfunctional our families were then. For me, being with her was fun, friendship, escape. I remember how we would laugh and have fun. I was a soprano and she an alto,

so we'd play our guitars and make up songs. I still have copies of those songs. I got to do things with her and her family that my 15 family never did. I remember spending Easter vacation in Palm Springs; I'll never forget that. We had so much fun by the pool flirting with the boys.

"The years went by; her family started going to a different church. We met up again in college. After college, we kept in touch by writing, phone calls, and occasionally meeting. For long periods of time we would not see each other, and yet when we met we would pick up where we left off. We gained a better understanding of each other as we gained a better understanding of ourselves, realizing the baggage we carried, trying to sort it all out as we lived our lives. Through all the years and phases, the bottom line is, we're friends, supporting each other through everything, every relationship, every parent, job, every-

thing. We've not only loved each other but liked each other, and we still have fun when we're together. And we still sing."

Surviving difficult family situations can be tough, if not impossible, to do alone. Often we can look back and point to one or two friends who offered us an escape or a point of sanity along the way. Marla and Dierdre, now in their forties, wonder what they would have done without each other when they were young, dealing with families that were filled with conflict and confusion.

Dierdre explained, "Our families were very different, yet very similar. We both had

many siblings, and sometimes things got a bit crazy at home. Marla and I created our own little world to escape the stress and angst of being prepubescent girls in large families. We made a playhouse that was our exclusive turf behind Marla's house. We created fantasy lives where we would reenact TV shows or

18

pretend we were married adult women and our husbands did this or that. We used to camp out there. As I look back now I realize I relied heavily on my friendship with Marla to bring order and sanity into my life."

Marla added, "Dierdre and I would play for hours in her room too. She had a record player and forty-fives and lots of neat stuff. My bedroom was off limits even to me except for sleeping. The sanctity of Dierdre's room was comforting to me."

Dierdre summarized, "Our friendship as young girls taught me that sometimes you need to go outside of your family to get what you need. I knew I could rely on Marla. And although our methods of coping today are much different than when we were children, I still gain strength and peace of mind from our friendship. No one understands me the way Marla does. Today, because of our history together, a phone call or a simple nod from my friend can put things in perspective."

Dr. Tina Tessina, author of *True Partners: A Workbook for Developing Lasting Intimacy*, echoes this essential component of friendship. "Friends are incredibly valuable. Relationships with friends are usually less stressful than relationships with family or love interests and therefore more supportive."[2] Certainly in times of trouble, girlfriends with whom we create a safe and sane reality can be the thin thread that pulls us through.

2. Quoted in Rosemarie Lennon, "Childhood Friends Shape Our Lives Forever," *For Women First*, July 3, 1995, 87.

Get a Grip!

SURELY WE OUGHT TO PRIZE THOSE
FRIENDS ON WHOSE PRINCIPLES AND
OPINIONS WE MAY CONSTANTLY RELY—
OF WHOM WE MAY SAY IN ALL
EMERGENCIES, "I KNOW WHAT THEY
WOULD THINK."

—*Hannah Farnham Lee (1844)*

Sometimes we need a friend to give us a kick
start to break out of a bad habit or a negative
way of looking at ourselves. When we need
to get a grip, a true girlfriend will offer help-
ful suggestions and, if ever necessary, she
will take charge. Annette, a management

consultant, says that the important thing is that the friend's impatience be wrapped in kindness and generosity, as illustrated by the following story told by one of the authors.

Tamara tells this story: "One night in college, I was studying for a calculus exam far into the night. Although I had enjoyed the class and working out the problems, all of a sudden I froze and could not absorb anything. My heart was racing. I went back to my dorm room and began fairly bubbling hysteria to my roommate. I was pacing and literally wringing my hands, while she sat and watched me over her glasses and book. 23

"'Tamara,' her voice cut through, 'there is a bottle of Scotch in the closet left over from our last party. I want you to pick up that glass, go over to the closet, pour yourself a shot, and drink it.' I just stared at her; was she crazy? I was studying for a calculus exam, for heaven's sake. 'Just do it,' she commanded. And I did it. As the Scotch burned its way down my throat, it seemed to cut a hole right through the panic. I just looked at her dumbly and said, 'Thanks, I needed that.' I felt like I was in the old aftershave ad. And, happy ending, I got an A on the exam. Thank God for Betsy."

Sally, a first-time author, described how she went through a meltdown at the thought of seeing her name in print. She told us, "I was just wigging out. I was completely convinced that I had written something totally stupid and everyone who saw it was going to think I was the most ridiculous person on earth. I would lie awake at night and stare at the ceiling and worry, night after night after night. Finally my girl-friend said, 'You know this isn't real, don't 25 you?' She validated my feelings but didn't let me get away with my weird thinking. As soon as I recognized my feelings for what they were, the whole thing sort of went away. I am so grateful to her for that."

At other times, we may need someone to support us in our decisions and help us to clarify our thinking if we get muddled in the process of living them out. If it weren't for our friends to observe, comment, and encourage, would any of us make changes in our lives? Laurie, a graduate student,

talks about her experience: "I am making a transition from a career as an investment banker, which was not my life's calling, to a career as a psychologist, which I believe is my life's calling. In gaining strength and courage enough to make the transition, I am forever indebted to Lisa, who knew me and believed in me more than I knew and believed in myself."

Sometimes love is soft and sweet, nice and nurturing. But often the love that is needed is strong, confrontive, and clear. Sentimentality is tossed aside for the penetrating vision of someone who knows us well 27 and cares enough to take us on. When we are confused, we can rely on these girlfriends to point the way to clarity and maybe even to give us the necessary boot to get started.

Soul Connection

THERE ARE THESE HUGE THUNDER
STORMS, AND WE SIT OUT ON THE
PORCH IN ROCKING CHAIRS WITH
COFFEE AND TALK, AND COMES THE
DAWN.

—*Robin Williams*

Some friendships are so strong, they
become part of us; they become visceral.
"We're in each other's blood," says Gina of
her friend Faith and herself; they have been
friends for thirty-five years since they grew
up in southern Wisconsin. Rachel Anne, a
retired teacher in her early seventies, reveals

the formula for maintaining a life-long friendship with her friend Joyce even though she has moved and changed over the years of her life: "There's no real secret about it; it's just that our lives crossed in a very meaningful way.  Our mothers were friends, we had a lot of basic common experiences, we graduated from the same high school, and so forth. She still lives on the shores of Lake Okoboji, where I grew up and where my great-grandfather homesteaded. Generation after generation of contacts means that, even when time and space have intervened, there's still a lot of basic shared fabric."

Common experience can cultivate a soul connection between women. Susan, book industry executive and mother of two daughters, told us about Jeanette, also a single mother who lives about eight blocks from her home. Susan said, "Jeanette is about the same

age that I am, coincidentally has two daughters, and our girls are friends with each other. We are both divorced, and we've had a lot of shared experiences. She has listened to me when I've ranted and raved about things, and I've listened to her do the same. We carpool, the girls take swimming lessons together, and we do various other activities together. We're  always available to each other. We also have nearly the same birthday—hers is May twenty-first and mine is May twenty-second."

Sometimes you become so connected with a friend that other people mistake you for each other. Perhaps they have merely linked your names in their minds because you are with your friend frequently, or perhaps there is a more ephemeral reason: When two people share an intuitive link, other people unconsciously pick up that link. Anne, an early childhood educator, recalled such an incident involving her friend: "I was walking down the street one day and ran into a man who was a mutual friend of mine and of a college friend. We said hello, and he exclaimed, 'Oh, Shirley, you've had your baby!' I walked on, completely bewildered, for about a block, until I realized he was talking about my college friend Shirley!"

Sometimes we become so identified with a friend that we begin noticing we have both clicked into the same mental track. Martha, a homemaker from Pennsylvania, described "tracking" her friend: "In high school, when we were closest, we were so in sync that we didn't need to verbalize our thoughts some of the time. We frequently showed up wearing the same or similar outfits." Helen, a songwriter, has had the same experience with her friend  Marianne: "We think so much alike sometimes that once we bought identical sequined blouses without the other's knowledge."

And then there are the physical connections, which are sometimes eerie and always unexplainable. For instance, when Marianne broke her right ankle and Helen broke her left ankle just one week apart, their husbands thought they'd taken this female bonding a bit far. And Tamara, one of the authors, tells this story: "After years of talking, planning, and dreaming, my

friend Laura and I both left our careers as lawyers in large, corporate law firms. Both of us were pursuing our dreams; she wanted to be a theatrical producer, and I had decided to get involved in publishing. She was producing her very first play on Broadway, and it was opening to much critical acclaim. I was invited to the opening of the play and was so proud of my friend; to have accomplished so much in so little time underscored the hard-won belief that one did not have to be afraid of pursuing one's dreams. I was thrilled to see her there, in the middle of all that attention, but I felt somewhat puzzled (and impressed) that she seemed so calm and relaxed. I became completely absorbed in the play, but as the closing scene began, I felt an overwhelming sense of nausea. I missed the last scene as I rushed to the bathroom to throw up! When I told her about my misfortune, she understood immediately and thanked me for getting sick for her. We both knew exactly what had happened."

Darlene, a psychotherapist, describes what she calls the "soul connection" she has

with a couple of women friends. She explains, "Our bond defies time. Our paths may not cross for the longest time, but when we get back together it's like no time has passed. We have enough common interests and a willingness to be real—to get to that level where you really share what's going on in your mind and your heart. I guess the back-and-forthness of it is really valuable, especially to me, since as a therapist I spend so much time listening. It's so nice to be able to blab and have somebody listen to me for a change. But it's really the intensity and completeness within a moment that gives us such a soul connection."

Some women refer to a male lover as a soulmate, and yet sharing that kind of bond with another woman brings its own unique pleasures. There are certain things that

38 never have to be explained to a female friend—the essence of being a woman at this point in history. A soul connection can develop from different points of commonality. Rachel Anne and Joyce and Susan and Jeanette built their soul connections on common life experiences. Helen and Marianne shared an almost psychic connection while Tamara and Laura bonded through launching major life transitions at the same time. This common knowledge, on an experiential, intuitive, or even psychic level, can bond us powerfully and forever.

Friend as Counselor

WHAT DO WE LIVE FOR, IF IT IS NOT
TO MAKE LIFE LESS DIFFICULT FOR
EACH OTHER?

—*George Eliot (c. 1850)*

~

One aspect of the age in which we live is
that many people see psychotherapists or
counselors. People who in past decades
would have gone to visit their minister or
rabbi or consulted an older, wiser member
of the family now may visit a counselor to
work through their problems. One woman
commented that therapy could be considered "paid friendship" and that if we had a

good circle of caring friends who were good listeners, we'd have less need to rely on professional therapists.

Of course, friendship will not solve all psychological ills. But for the day-to-day counseling, the reciprocal listening without judgment, our friends can be invaluable. Janice, thirty-seven, describes her experience: "We can listen to each other in a nonjudgmental way. The other day, my friend, who is working in her husband's family business, called me and said she had yelled at her brother-in-law while at work. She had been loud, and she felt awful about how she had handled herself. Her husband was upset with  her too. We have shared many ugly stories about ourselves, and usually we just need to have someone hear about whatever happened. This time, however, I offered some advice. My friend called her brother-in-law, and they had a very productive conversation. That's just one of many examples of how we help each other."

Friends often provide a listening ear over the phone. Something about the telephone allows us to fully unburden ourselves. It is the modern confessional, the dark booth in which we are alone and yet not alone, where we can spill out the things about which we are most ashamed. By not having to face a friend, we can get the dark secrets or unexplainable feelings out. Seventeen-year-old Molly told us, "When I'm talking about a difficult subject, it's just easier not to actually be there looking at her. I can't really see her reaction, so I can just tell my story without being inhibited. I'm much more relaxed and able to talk openly when I'm on the phone." 43

One of the most valuable characteristics of a counselor is confidentiality. Contrary to the myths of popular culture whereby women are supposedly unable to keep a secret, we found that confidentiality is an attribute most appreciated and respected by women. Over and over again, women responded to the question of what characteristics they valued most about a friend with "the ability

to keep a secret." As Patty, a homemaker 44 from southern Illinois, says, "We all know that we have things that happen in our lives that we don't want everyone to know but that we need to vent or talk about. I can't stress enough how I value people keeping a secret."

Sometimes we tell a friend our secret because we need to try it out on someone and learn if we can still be accepted by her. Janet, a sales manager, says the closeness of a friendship is defined by the ability to "know the dark side of someone and love her anyway." Rene, a resource teacher, explains, "I can express my dreams, fantasies, or fears without anxiety because I know they will remain in confidence and I won't be considered crazy. I can pick up the phone and call my friend Eleanor, even if it's just to say, 'I just needed to say this out loud to someone.' I know she will listen with love and acceptance, giving me her perspective if I ask for it or just lending a listening ear."

Perhaps KC, a dancer and choreographer, said it most vividly: "One of the things I most admire about my friendship with Holly is that I can say even the ugly stuff about myself to her. I'm realizing how

important that is. I can say anything. I feel very free and very open and unjudged by Holly in this friendship, and that's a tremendous thing for me. I think we often spend a lot of time feeling guilty about the negative things that we think inside, but they're part of us and they're also passing through us. I value being able to express that to somebody without her saying, 'Oh, yuck, you think that, or you feel that?' That's very valuable."

FRIEND AS COUNSELOR

No one knows why feeling accepted completely, faults and all, is so powerfully healing. We just know that we are trans- 47 formed when someone else listens to us, taking in our experience. For the listening ear, the assurance of confidentiality, and the well-placed word of advice, we thank our women friends.

Refreshment

THOSE WHO ARE UNHAPPY HAVE NO
NEED FOR ANYTHING IN THIS WORLD
BUT PEOPLE CAPABLE OF GIVING THEM
ATTENTION.

—Simone Weil

We go to our friends for nourishment, both
figuratively and literally. Kristine, a house
cleaner from Minnesota, says that what she
most appreciates about getting together with
her friends is that she can "come with all baggage attached and leave feeling refreshed and
energized." Patricia describes time spent with
her friends as "time out, total relaxation."

What kind of magic happens with our friends? A simple magic: a shared cup of tea, a walk on the beach or around the block, just connection. Replenishment can be an easy thing. Arlene, an author, lyrically describes the pleasures of spending time with her friend Margit, a yoga teacher, where they both come away mutually replenished, spiritually and physically: "The morning is dreary. Rain clouds gathering. I rested fitfully last night, and so I feel

drained of energy, head foggy, bones achy. She's as cheery as ever, having a cup of tea. Later we start to make lunch. The rhythms are natural. She

starts the preparations while I read something she has written. I take over the season-
ing of the soup and the final touches while
she reads something I have written. The com-
bination of our two efforts makes our writing,
as well as our soup, more interesting to both

of us than our usual individual attempts. And we both cherish each other's viewpoints and suggestions in the lunch conversation. We also both know when we are full—satisfied, nourished, heart, stomach, soul, body—and it's time to say good-bye and take the refreshed energy back into our own work."

One woman explained how a most thoughtful friend helped her through several difficult times in her life "by merely insisting that I join various dinner parties at her house. When my heart had been trampled in the dust by a love affair gone awry, when I was feeling so trapped in my career I thought I would explode, I had a tendency to hole up in my apartment, cry, and eat junk food. The problems would seem to get big-

ger and bigger (as would I) as I sat there
alone.

"She would call at the right time, and I
would pour out my problems. After listening carefully and calmly, she, an inveterate
hostess, would say, 'I think you should come
over to my house for dinner tonight.' I
would wail in return, 'I'm not hungry, I've
been eating junk food all day, and I'm in too
bad a mood.' She would insist that I needed
to be around some people and then would

request that I come over early to 'help her cook.' Helping her cook, I would realize, often meant that I would stir the risotto while she plied me with sherry and made me realize that my problems would not destroy me and the world was not falling apart after all."

53

Replenishment can also result in a change of life's focus. Carmen, one of the authors and a massage and body worker in Southern California, credits her friend Bobette with intro-ducing her to the benefits of massage over a decade ago. She said, "I was what I now call 'a

walking head.' I was totally out of touch
with my body. Then Bobette talked me into
54 going to a hot springs one summer and trying out a mud bath and massage. I would
never have gone if she hadn't put the trip all
together. There we were, floating in mud,
sipping our water from straws, and having
the time of our lives. And then I had my first
massage. Whooooosh! What a surprise to
find I had a body! That day marked a new
era for me personally and professionally,
and all because Bobette insisted I try something new!"

Often we can view relaxing or taking care
of ourselves as a luxury. But the refreshment
of body and spirit, available through our connections with other women, can add years to

our lives, replenish us after a dry period, or even start a new phase of life. Our friends can rejuvenate us by just letting us be, or they may drag our tired spirits and bodies, frequently protesting, to a place (physical or mental) where we will be renewed.

Acceptance

OH, THE COMFORT, THE INEXPRESS-
IBLE COMFORT OF FEELING SAFE WITH
A PERSON, HAVING NEITHER TO WEIGH
THOUGHTS NOR MEASURE WORDS, BUT
POURING THEM ALL RIGHT OUT, JUST
AS THEY ARE, CHAFF AND GRAIN
TOGETHER; CERTAIN THAT A FAITHFUL
HAND WILL TAKE AND SIFT THEM,
KEEP WHAT IS WORTH KEEPING, AND
THEN WITH THE BREATH OF KINDNESS
BLOW THE REST AWAY.

—*Dinah Maria Mulock Craik*

The best thing about girlfriends is that we can be whoever we are with them, and they will accept us anyway. No persona required, we can be cranky or perky—and both may be annoying—with greasy hair and a sweater two sizes too small that's covered with ugly little balls. It really does not matter to our close friends what we look like or what mood we're in. As Alice describes

being with her friends, there are "no holds barred, no image making or trying to live up to an ideal." Cheryl observes, "When you're with your really good friends you don't care what you look like. Each year my friends and I take a trip away from our families. In the mornings, everyone just walks around looking as though they are eighty years old. No one is trying to impress anyone else. Competition is not a part of our friendship."

Judy Hart, the author of *Love, Judy: Letters of Hope and Healing for Women with Breast Cancer*, most appreciates those friends who are not afraid of her

sickness and her feelings around it. Having friends accept her in whatever mental and physical state she happens to be in is very important. "The most crucial form of friendship for me has been what I call my psyche friends. Obviously there are people who will do an errand for you or take you to an appointment, leave something on the doorstep, send something in the mail, telephone. But the

women who have really made the difference for me are the ones I can talk to absolutely from where I am and who are not going to be shocked or tell me to feel better or give me advice. I'm most touched by those who have been courageous enough to share what my illness means to them.

"I guess opening up the passages is a lot of what I'm doing with the cancer, because I know it is a threatening subject, and I was brought up in a time, a place, a family where you're not supposed to talk about unpleasant things unless you can be upbeat. The image that I grew up with is people 61 talking about somebody who lost her husband saying, 'Oh, she's just wonderful. She gets her hair done, she gets a nice suit of clothes, she takes a cruise to Europe, and she plays bridge with the girls.' What they really mean is that she's not making anyone uncomfortable that she's going through anything different or unusual or difficult. I'd rather be real, and a part of me inside says, 'Oh, you're breaking all the rules,' and then I watch how it does open up the passages. But I think this is what friendships and human relationships are all about— daring to keep open the passages."

By accepting characteristics of friends, we may find that we are achieving a balance 62 in our own lives. Sue Thoele and Bonnie Hampton each feel that the other has brought some balance to her development. Bonnie noted, "I spent the formative years of my life, 1960 to 1981, in Berkeley, living an avant garde, California lifestyle. There was a kind of independence and toughness about me that Sue didn't have. There was an intu-

itive womanliness about her that I didn't have. We were able to tug each other into a balanced place around that. When

we get out of balance we can reach out, and the other person helps balance that out. It's just completeness."

Sue continues, "What keeps coming up in my mind, because I am really visual, is the yin-yang symbol. When we met, I had an incredible amount of yin energy, and

Bonnie had such an incredible amount of yang energy. We were imbalanced. Our relationship helped us stabilize and balance and harmonize those energies in ourselves."

By feeling accepted, we learn to like ourselves more. When we like ourselves more, we can accept others and be more patient about what we think of as their foibles. By

being more accepting of our friends, we may bring some balance into our own lives. The cycle that friendship provides is a worthwhile one to begin.

Helping Us Change (Even When We'd Rather Not)

TO ACT THE PART OF A TRUE FRIEND
REQUIRES MORE CONSCIENTIOUS FEEL-
ING THAN TO FILL WITH CREDIT AND
COMPLACENCY ANY OTHER STATION
OR CAPACITY IN SOCIAL LIFE.
—*Sarah Ellis (1834)*

Sometimes our friends recognize it is time
for us to be in transition before we do. True
friends help us grow, even when we'd pre-

fer to stay right where we are. Lynn told us that a friend helped her to find her voice again, literally, after injury and malice had caused her to lose it. She had been a voice major in college, when she came under the unscrupulous tutelage of a teacher who was secretly jealous of the young women she taught. Following this voice teacher's malicious instructions, Lynn developed nodules on her vocal cords and could no longer sing.

Lynn told us, "For years, I wouldn't sing 67 at all. Nothing. The music had gone out of me. Debby, one of my lifelong friends, took it upon herself to get me to sing, but she knew me well enough to know that I can be quite a stubborn woman. So she tricked me. We'd be driving in her car, and she'd start singing a simple song like 'Jesus Loves Me,' and before long I'd be singing along with her. Then she'd sing a more difficult song, and without my realizing it, I'd sing that one too. After a while, I was singing up a storm!

She knew me so well that she knew I needed to get my voice back and that she'd have to be clever in how she helped me. Now that's a real friend!" 69

Deciding when to push a friend and when to hold back can be complicated, and all a woman can do is use her unique knowledge of that friend to make the decision. Sandra, a teacher, told this story of when her friend Ellen was in a violent relationship: "Ellen said that her other friends were just saying, 'Get out of there!' which was exactly my gut reac-

tion. However, I said to her things like, 'I'm sure you would, if you could,' 'I see you laying your stepping-stones.' I realized I had to put trust in her and help her have trust and confidence in her own process. I began to see and reflect for her that she was taking steps and that she had some kind of a trustworthy process.

"She did get out, and I felt I offered a dif-

ferent voice than other people who also really cared about her and were also perfectly right in being blunt. It's a tricky business knowing when you

say it all and when you don't. Because that's the risk—you don't know. You don't know whether you haven't shown enough courage if you don't say it all, you don't know if you're not going to help by not saying it all. Very subtle."

Caring enough to get your hands dirty,

72 even when you aren't asked for help, is the sign of a genuine friend. We might want our friends to leave us to our old ways, but these are

the friends we need most when we get stuck. Dinah Shore wisely said, "Trouble is a part of your life, and if you don't share it, you don't give the person who loves you enough chance to love you enough."[3]

3. Ibid., 44.

The Test of Time

THE GROWTH OF TRUE FRIENDSHIP
MAY BE A LIFELONG AFFAIR.
—*Sarah Orne Jewett (c. 1885)*

Some friendships last, no matter what changes each party makes. This durability seems to come from the shared ability to mature and to be interested in growing as individuals. Arlene talks about how her friendship with Ellie has lasted through periods of great personal trauma for each of them, as well as through the shifting of attitudes and perceptions about themselves as people: "Our friendship spanned twenty-five years. Part of our relationship was based in a period of time when we were each trying to individuate from our husbands, who were very well known in their communities and in their respective industries. We were very supportive of each other. She introduced me to meditation, and

we got more involved in the process of developing our spiritual natures. She and her family ended up moving close to where I lived, and we did a lot of inner exploration together, going on these spiritual journeys together. Then things got better in both of our lives.

"Oddly, if you're there to support some- body in their neurosis or in their crisis, the friendship may not make the transition when things get better. But we've been able to shift into different gears all the way along the life of our friendship."

Asked why she thought this was so, Arlene replied, "Well, I think that our basic ways of looking at the world are of interest to each

other. And there was enough parallel experience that there was a good foundation. When her son was killed in an accident several years ago, she knew I had been through the experience of losing my son. I could be a resource for her, be there for her in ways

that a lot of people couldn't. And so that was a very valuable time. There was something very important that I had to give.

"When she came out of that grief, we started discussing this idea in which we both had always been interested: 'How do you give form to the creative process?' This gave us direction, because we've always felt out of step with others around us. Her husband is a larger-than-life character, and my husband created his business from scratch and has always been very focused. Ellie's and my minds didn't move that way. Ellie

and I had nonlinear lives, and there was no single direction in our work."

Friendships, like the one between Arlene and Ellie, survive for two reasons. One is that the friends share enough similarity in experience that they can identify and empathize with the other. The far more important reason however—the absence of which destroys many relationships—is the desire and ability to grow and stretch with each other in mutual development as human beings. When we make room for each other to mature, change, explore, and experiment, we make room for friendship that can stand the tests of time.

Acknowledgments

*Many thanks to those who
contributed photographs:*

Lisa Ashcraft

Joan Becker

Polly Blair

Marilyn Caldwell

Janice Carter

Carol Coe

Janet Couch

Kelly Cremens

Armen Davis

Lori Eberhardy

Vivian Elbert

Jennifer Fox

Erin Friedrich

Amy Garcia

Tamara Haus

Julie Herren

Margaret Hood

Susan Hood

JuJu Johnson

Maryetta Jones

Angee Kerrigan

Jessica Kerrigan

Lisa Martin

Susan Miller

Kristin Norell

Dorothy O'Brien

Jeanne Oliver

Patty Rice

Ellen Sadler

Leola Specht

Jean Spreen

Stephanie Vande Haar

Ella Vest

Marty Wellington

anything

& I would

at any

my

friends.

up,

a

nels

that

from

real

you

real